W. S Greenfield

Alcohol, its use and abuse

W. S Greenfield

Alcohol, its use and abuse

ISBN/EAN: 9783743373808

Manufactured in Europe, USA, Canada, Australia, Japa

Cover: Foto ©Lupo / pixelio.de

Manufactured and distributed by brebook publishing software (www.brebook.com)

W. S Greenfield

Alcohol, its use and abuse

HEALTH PRIMERS.

ALCOHOL:

ITS USE AND ABUSE.

BY

W. S. GREENFIELD, M. D.

NEW YORK:
D. APPLETON AND COMPANY,
1, 3, AND 5 BOND STREET.
1887.

CONTENTS.

	PAGE
INTRODUCTION	5
ALCOHOL AND ALCOHOLIC BEVERAGES	8
THE PHYSIOLOGICAL ACTION OF ALCOHOL	18
THE EFFECTS OF ALCOHOL WHEN TAKEN IN EXCESS	32
THE USES OF ALCOHOL AND ALCOHOLIC BEVERAGES	61
ALCOHOL IN ILL-HEALTH AND DISEASE	79
THE RIGHT USE OF ALCOHOL	92

ALCOHOL:
ITS USE AND ABUSE.

INTRODUCTION.

THE attempt to present in a popular form a subject on which so much has been said and written, on which so great a variety of opinion exists, and by which such strong feelings and prejudices are excited, as that of the use of alcohol, may by many be considered a rash one. But seeing how important the subject is to the general health and welfare of the community, and how little real influence our store of medical and physiological knowledge has had upon the habits of our countrymen, notwithstanding the eminence and ability of those who have written upon the subject, it seems to be a duty to endeavour to place the more important facts within the reach of all in a simple form.

There is no subject relating to health which has a greater practical importance, nor any on which more misconceptions exist. In a perfect community, governed by pure religion, morality, and intelligence, with no artificial habits, and no passions or vices, the use of intoxicating liquors would need no check; but in our actual state, all experience shows the dangers which may and do result from their abuse. But, as an example of the many wrong ideas which exist as to what excess is, there are few, except medical men, who know what serious injury may be done by drinking which hardly ever approaches intoxication, and which may be unrecognised by a man's nearest friends. We shall try to show what is the evil of drinking, and how to avoid it, what the good and how to gain it, without joining in a universal condemnation of the use of alcohol.

In the limits of our space we can only touch on the great questions involved; we must leave for the medical profession the study of the accumulated stores of scientific observation on the use of alcohol and the results of its abuse, from which we shall only draw such facts as may seem to be most useful for our purpose; nor can we even refer more than cursorily to the views of those whose scientific and moral eminence lends weight to their opinion as to the usefulness or injuriousness of alcohol. But we shall endeavour to give such reference to more extensive works as may prove of service to those who seek the higher fountainheads of information.

Nor let it be supposed that because we do not advocate or condemn total abstinence, we are to be counted either amongst its opponents or supporters, or that we are blind to the great moral importance of the teetotal question. We believe that an intelligent comprehension of the action of alcohol on the system will always have greater influence with thoughtful men in promoting temperance than any adhesion to a dogma. Moreover, we have no doubt that the moral and social arguments for total abstinence, which are after all its strongest weapons, but which lie beyond the province of our subject, will be strengthened by a calm consideration of what we know of the effects of alcohol in health and disease.

It will be our endeavour to regard the subject mainly from a scientific and practical point of view, to state what is known of the effects of alcohol on the body, the results of its abuse, and the right occasions and methods of its use, and to draw only such conclusions as are warranted by experience on the ground of preservation of health, avoiding the numerous other topics which arise in connexion with the subject of drinking.

Our subject being Alcohol : its use and abuse, we may first ask what alcohol is, in what way it is usually taken, and how much is contained in ordinary drinks. Then we may examine its action on the healthy system, and see what powers it possesses—its so-called *physiological* action. Further, we shall see what is its effect when taken in excess, either for a time or habitually. And, finally, having seen what good it can effect and what mischief it may do, we shall be in a position to study its use in health or disease, and draw such general inferences as may guide us in our ordinary habits.

CHAPTER I.

ALCOHOL AND ALCOHOLIC BEVERAGES.

NEARLY all the intoxicating drinks used by man depend for their peculiar properties on the presence of a substance known to chemists as *alcohol*. This is associated in many cases with other bodies called *ethers*, which are also intoxicating, and it is more or less largely diluted with water, and combined or mixed with various substances which give colour, taste, and smell, or which are nutritious, such as sugar and starchy bodies, or which have other chemical properties. The amount of alcohol in drinks (to be more precisely stated later) varies from 1 part in 70 (in small beer) to more than 1 in 2 (in strong whisky); but it can equally be obtained from all by distillation.

Pure alcohol as obtained by the chemist is a colourless volatile liquid, with a faint pleasant odour and but little taste. It is lighter in weight than water, its specific gravity being 796, boiling at 172° Fahr., and it is not frozen by a cold of −166° Fahr. If a few drops of it be placed on the hand it evaporates, producing a sensation of cold and slight tingling. It readily burns with a colourless flame. It has a strong attraction for water, so that, if in a moist atmosphere, it dilutes itself by combining with water; and if cold pure alcohol and water are mixed, slight warmth is produced by their combination. On account of this property, and of preventing putrefaction, strong spirit is used to preserve animal and vegetable bodies and tissues, such as the various creatures seen in museum jars, fruits for the housewife, &c. And it very rapidly dries out the water from anything with which it comes in contact.

Chemists tell us that this common or "ethylic" alcohol is made up of three elements, carbon, hydrogen, and oxygen, and they represent its composition by the formula C_2H_6O. When burnt with air or oxygen, it produces water and a substance called carbonic acid, which is identical with one of the gases constantly breathed out from our lungs; formed, too, by burning coal, gas, oil, or wood, charcoal, or coke, &c., and which is the substance in the air which makes it impure, unfit for breathing, and necessitates ventilation.*

In whatever shape it is found naturally alcohol always results from the process of fermentation of substances containing sugar; and though the chemist can, by complicated processes, build it up in small quantities out of its original elements, this need not enter into our calculations. To prepare pure alcohol from any of these fermentation products repeated distillation and other means

* For other chemical details see works on Chemistry.

of purification are necessary, to free it from other volatile substances and also from water, which it holds with great tenacity; but strong spirits (containing from 70 to 90 per cent. of alcohol) can be obtained pretty readily.

For purposes of diet, alcohol is always used in combination, and the majority of liquors contain a considerable number of other substances, held in solution by water; and the alcohol is probably combined more or less intimately with these other ingredients. The more important bodies are called "ethers"—bodies allied to alcohol, and also formed in fermentation or by subsequent chemical changes in the alcohol. It is to these that most of the special odours and "bouquet" of wines and spirits are due; and they give peculiar stimulating and intoxicating powers to some wines, even when in small quantity. Other "alcohols," differing in composition, but analogous in nature to ethylic alcohol, "*methylic*," "*amylic*," &c., are produced in small quantity in some fermentations; e.g., amylic alcohol is the "fusel oil" which constitutes an impurity in whisky. They are all more deleterious than ethylic alcohol, and have special poisonous properties.

Besides these, the liquor contains usually colouring matter, and more or less starchy and saccharine matter, with various saline bodies, such as common salt, salt of tartar, &c., and some essential oils. To give in any detail the various constituents of each and their proportion would much exceed our limits. In a general way we may say that spirits, brandy, whisky, and gin, contain, if pure, no starch and very little sugar; rum, more sugar; wines, chiefly saccharine and saline bodies with ethers and essential oils; ale, stout, and porter, much starchy and "extractive" matter.

Amount of Alcohol in various Liquors.—This is the most important practical point for our purpose. Later we must consider the other ingredients and their action.

The following table gives the average percentage of alcohol in some of the commoner beverages :— *

Whisky	50 to 60	Claret—	
Brandy	50 to 60	Strongest Bordeaux	17
Rum	60 to 77	Mean	15
Gin	49 to 60	Vin ordinaire	8 or 9
Port Wine—		Champagne	5 to 13
		Hock	9 to 12
Strongest	25	Sauterne	14
Ordinary	23	Cider	5 to 10
Weakest	16·5	Ale —	
Madeira	16 to 22	Burton	9
		Ordinary	3 to 5
Sherry—		Perry	7
Strongest	25	Brown Stout	6 to 7
Weakest	16	London Porter	4·2
Burgundy	10 to 14	London Small Beer	1·28

* The statements here are taken from the most recent and trustworthy sources. There is a good deal of difference in the

It is only right to say that this table gives only approximate results, for the quantity of alcohol in wines or beers of the same name differs very greatly; there is no fixed standard. Perhaps the most useful way of putting the quantity of alcohol is to say how many ounces of the beverage contain about one ounce of alcohol. The largest quantity of alcohol which can be taken per diem without evident ill effects is, according to Dr. Parkes, $1\frac{1}{2}$ oz.

From our table we see that 1 ounce would be contained in about 4 or 5 ounces of port or sherry, and from 6 to 10 ounces of claret or hock, and 12 to 20 of ale or stout. The varying size of wine-glasses renders any certain statement as to the number of glasses which make up this amount impossible; but two glasses of port or sherry, or two or three glasses of claret, represent it pretty nearly. Half a pint of Burton ale, or a pint of ordinary ale, would nearly contain it. Some of the lighter ales and common porter contain much less. Hence, for $1\frac{1}{2}$ ounce of alcohol, we may reckon three or four glasses of port or sherry; three to five of claret; two glasses of Burton ale; one and

---

figures given by different authorities. The amount is here given by *volume*, not by weight. It is idle to give decimals when the percentage is so variable. For other tables showing the analysis of a large number of wines, &c., and for more accurate calculations, see Thudichum and Dupré ('Origin, Nature, and Use of Wines,' 1872).

a half to two pints of common ale; and perhaps two to three pints of the very weakest ale. But we must bear in mind that this is the outside limit, and represents the quantity which just fails to produce any obvious diminution of work in healthy men; whether it does not cause some deterioration of the organs is another question.

But it is not merely the amount of alcohol which is important; its action is partly controlled by its state of combination. A pint of brandy-and-water, of such strength as to contain only as much alcohol as a pint of beer, will yet act somewhat differently; and there are other substances in beers and wines which variously influence both nutrition and digestion.

The composition and special properties of some of these may with advantage be briefly reviewed.

Beer.—An average sample of beer contains in 20 ounces (1 pint)—

Alcohol	1 oz.
Extractives, dextrine, and sugar	1·2 ,, (524 grains)
Free acid (lactic, acetic, gallic, and malic acid)	25 grains.
Salts (alkaline chlorides and phosphates)	13 ,,
Carbonic acid and volatile and essential oils.	

Porter contains caramel (burnt sugar), and usually more dextrine and sugar than ale.

Special action of Beers.—According to Dr. Parkes, the special physiological action of beer is to lessen the excretion (removal by the organs) of the products of tissue change, both *urea*, the waste nitrogen product carried off by the kidneys, and carbonic acid, the waste carbon product given off from the lungs. This action is not due to the alcohol contained, but to some other substance.

A daily excess of beer, as all know, leads to a state of fulness and plethora, and a great accumulation of fat. This is partly due to a check in the proper nutritive changes in the tissues, partly to increased supply of fat-forming substances. The waste products are imperfectly burnt off, and accumulate in the system, giving rise to gouty and bilious disorders.

The use of beer in moderation answers several purposes besides the action of the alcohol: it supplies substances which are nutrient and fat-forming, and lessens the destruction of fat, and thus increases the weight of the body. The free acids and the bitter extractive matters, which are chiefly derived from the hops, are useful as stomachic tonics and serve to promote digestion. The salts also assist in nutrition, though in what manner we do not know. In moderation, therefore, beer is undoubtedly useful to many.

Wines.—Wines, as we have said, vary very greatly in their composition, and so widely, that we could not give even the average composition of any one sort of wine to serve any useful purpose.

Wines alter much by keeping; they undergo important chemical changes. Red wines contain a good deal of tannin, derived from the grape-skins; this is in great part precipitated with some colouring matter; and tartrate of potash is also gradually precipitated. Some of the sugar undergoes complex chemical changes, and with the alcohol forms ethers, which give bouquet to the wine; part also of the alcohol is lost by gradual evaporation. Hence old wine is much less rich in sugar and alcohol, and contains less astringent and saline matter than young and fruity wine, but more ethers. Hence the properties of any given wine alter very much with age.

Although the chemical constitution of the alcohol contained in wines is the same as that in spirits, there can be no doubt that the action is very different from that of spirits, as we have already said. Tissue degeneration is much less readily produced when the alcohol is thus taken.

The vegetable salts contained in wine, especially in the natural light red wines, serve in some cases a very useful purpose. According to Dr. Parkes they are highly "anti-scorbutic," that is, they prevent the occurrence of scurvy. Scurvy is produced by the want of vegetable salts, which, either by fresh vegetables or juice of fruits (e.g., lime-juice), must be supplied to the body. "In a campaign the issue of red wines should never be omitted." (Parkes.)

The ethers have peculiar rapid stimulant qualities, and they are believed to promote the absorption of fat by exciting the secretion of the *pancreas*, one of the organs which manufactures a digestive fluid which especially acts upon fat. According to the late Dr. Anstie, the ethers are of especial value as stimulants in diseases of children, and to aged persons.

A great deal of the difference in digestibility of wines depends upon the quantity of sugar and free acids and acid salts. The tannin also has a peculiar astringent effect, which in some cases aids, in others deranges digestion.

It would be easy to say a great deal about the effects popularly attributed to various liquors, and with some show of reason. Science certainly lags behind experience in this matter, as in many others. We know more of the effects of liquor upon disease and in producing disease than of some other actions. Gin and whisky have a peculiar action upon the kidneys and skin, because they contain certain substances in addition to alcohol which act upon those organs; pale brandy is more beneficial in allaying sickness than is rum; rum fattens more than gin, and the like. We can at least give plausible reasons for these facts. Absinthe liqueur gives rise to a peculiar form of mania, and to epilepsy, which are accounted for by the direct action of the absinthe. But why is it that, as is asserted and maintained, not only by popular belief but by statistics, that in countries and districts in which white wine is produced and drunk there are far more crimes of violence under the influence of liquor than where red wine is habitually taken; that natural white wines have so different an action from red of equal alcoholic strength? And whence arises the belief, supported we believe by experience, that white wine is more "heating" than red?*

Nor have we space to do more than mention the varied mental effects produced by drinking different liquors. It is a popular belief that authors who take wine or spirits to promote the flow of thought and invention, and stimulate them in their work, have the mental product coloured by the kind of stimulant they take. Poets have from early ages been charged with the failing of drawing

* Those who make Alpine ascents will have noticed that steady guides usually take red wine to drink whilst on the climb, reserving a bottle of white wine to drink when the summit has been reached, and the party is resting exposed to cold air. They maintain that for warmth only is white wine to be taken. Those interested in practical experience should question some of the best Swiss guides as to the different action of wines and spirits. We have had some very interesting chats on the subject above the snow line.

inspiration from wine; and even the divine Homer has been called "Vinosus Homerus."* A like charge has been made against many poets since; in some cases, it must be feared with too much truth, in the cases of Byron, Campbell, and Edgar Allan Poe, for example. But we have no exact knowledge of the relative mental effects of different stimulants; we point it out only as a subject worthy of inquiry.

We may postpone the consideration of the choice of a beverage until we have further discussed the action of alcohol.

CHAPTER II.

THE PHYSIOLOGICAL ACTION OF ALCOHOL.

By this we mean its action on the body in a state of health—how it modifies the natural actions of life, such as the circulation, the power of feeling, movement, and

* . . . Si credis, . . .
 Nulla placere diu, nec vivere carmina possunt,
 Quæ scribuntur aquæ potoribus. . . .
  Laudibus arguitur vini vinosus Homerus:
 Ennius ipse pater nunquam nisi potus ad arma
 Prosiluit dicenda.
     HORACE, *Epist.* lib. i., xix. 1-9.

so on. And here we must only very briefly speak of some of the more important effects which are observed by experiment. Let any one who knows how many and various are the natural actions which go on in the body, consider what a multitude of effects such an agent as alcohol might produce in different doses, and he will see how complex the subject is. And we shall have to mention a great many of these effects again from time to time, so need not so fully discuss them here.

The effect of alcohol differs as it is given in a small dose, a repetition of small doses, or a large dose at once. The most important direct actions are upon the circulation of the blood, and upon the nervous system.

Absorption of Alcohol.—When alcohol is taken in any form into the stomach, it is taken up by the minute, so-called capillary, or hair-like blood-vessels which ramify in its structure; from them it gets into the larger vessels or veins, and is conveyed to the heart. The heart, as most people know, is the hollow muscular organ which propels the blood through the body. It is divided into two halves, and each of these again consists of two cavities or chambers, one of which, the *auricle*, first receives the blood, which then passes into the *ventricle*, which propels it into the arteries. The blood which comes from the veins of the body goes into the right auricle, and is sent on by the right ventricle into the lungs, where it passes through a network of capillary vessels in contact with the air, and is so purified, then it goes back to the left side of the heart, which sends it into the arteries of the body to do its work again. But all the blood which goes from the stomach passes first to the liver, which is interposed as a sort of sieve between the stomach and the heart. The minute vessels of the stomach unite into one large trunk, or vein, which joins the veins from the bowels; and when it reaches the liver breaks up again into an infinity of small branches, which ramify through the liver, and join again into one large trunk vessel, which carries the blood to the right side of the heart.

So that all the alcohol which we drink, after becoming diluted with water, is absorbed by the blood, carried to the liver, thence to the heart, then the lungs, back to the heart again, and is distributed from it to all parts of the body. If the alcohol is injected into the veins, it makes its way straight to the right side of the heart without going through the liver; if inhaled into the lungs as vapour, it is carried straight to the left side of the heart. But even when it takes the roundabout course through the liver to heart and lungs before it gets into the general blood-stream, it passes through in a very short time—not more than a minute or two—and its general effects are very rapidly produced. The absorption from the stomach continues as long as any more alcohol is present there, and its rate of absorption is modified by various conditions.

Alcohol, as such, cannot be taken up directly by the vessels, but must first be diluted with water in order to pass through their walls. Now when we take anything, especially solid food, into the stomach, one of the first effects is to produce a fulness of the blood-vessels of the lining or "mucous membrane" of that organ, and then from it is poured out fluid which mixes with the food taken, and "digests" it, that is, fits it for absorption. The mucous membrane is provided with many organs called glands, which make various substances which act chemically upon the food, and are mingled with the watery fluid poured out by the vessels. The quantity and quality of these constituents of the "gastric juice," or digesting fluid, are beautifully regulated in their supply by the nature of the substance taken into the stomach. If nothing but a liquid, such as wine or brandy, is taken, very little but water is poured out, the effect being much like that of touching the eye and making it water; this mixes with the wine, and when properly diluted, the combined fluid is taken up by the blood-vessels.

But if we take wine with food, the solid food is mixed with it, and, moreover, a much larger quantity of fluid is poured out by the stomach wall into its own cavity, owing to the presence of the food, so that the absorption of the wine is more gradual and it becomes more diluted.

If we could look into the stomach just after taking a glass of wine, we should see that its inner surface became bright red where the wine touched it—in fact, blushed as it were. The same would be the case if a piece of meat were taken, but the colour would probably be less intense, and less rapidly produced. We shall see that this effect of alcohol is one which is widespread and very important. So far it acts merely as an irritant, by coming in contact with the mucous membrane, just as, if we dropped it into the eye, it would make it red and watery; but when it gets into the blood, it produces a similar effect in a different way.

The mixture with food, then, makes the absorption slower, and so does mixture with water; for clearly, there is a greater quantity of fluid to be taken up, and it needs a longer time, and less is taken up in a given time. The combination of the alcohol also makes a considerable difference; in the form of spirits and water it is most readily diffused into the blood, and acts most rapidly; next as wine, and slowest as malt liquor. One apparent exception must be noticed. If raw spirits are taken in any considerable quantity, no effect whatever may be observed for some little time. Many cases are on record where men for a wager, or in a drunken frolic, have drunk a bottle of spirits. The effect may be, often is, sudden death; but it may be that for a quarter or half an hour nothing happens; then sudden unconsciousness, going on to a condition of stupor, sets in, and speedy death occurs. This peculiar effect seems to be due to a sort of paralysis of the stomach, which takes some little time to recover its natural function of absorption.

Effect on the Circulation.—If any sufficient quantity of alcohol is taken, we see a more marked effect. The face flushes, the skin seems warmer; there is a sense of being warmer. How is this explained? We know that all parts of the body are abundantly supplied with blood-vessels, the smallest of which, called capillaries, make up a great part of the textures. Every beat of the heart drives blood through these networks of minute vessels, and the quantity thus supplied depends, of course, partly upon the force of the heart and the frequency of the pulse. But the arteries, or vessels which carry the blood from the heart to the capillaries, are not rigid tubes; they are elastic, and they also are muscular, and can alter their size in accordance with the needs of the part they supply. We regulate the quantity of gas we burn in several ways: we may control it either at the metre, or on its way to the lamp, or at the lamp itself by the tap; and the Gas Company, too, can give it greater or less pressure, or check our supply at the main. Now, if instead of thus having several taps or stop-cocks at intervals along our system of gas-pipes, we could arrange for the pipes to be narrowed at pleasure in their whole length, so as to make the channel smaller when we wanted less gas, and to dilate and get larger when we wanted more, we should have the same arrangement which is found in the blood-vessels. Suppose, too, that for the words "nervous system" we substituted "gas-engineer"; for "heart," "central gas-works," and for "arteries," "gas-pipes," and understood that the gas-engineer could, by means of electric wires, control the size of our gas-pipes, we should have a rough simile of the arrangement of our vessels. We must imagine also that the householder has the power of controlling his gas-pipes as well as the engineer. The arteries, even to their most minute branches, or *arterioles*, have this property of contracting and dilating, and they do this either in response to a central order conveyed by nerves, or in consequence of a local action upon their nerves, or their muscular coats. Alcohol has a very marked power of thus causing the vessels to dilate whenever it is contained in the blood, so that these minute vessels become turgid, and the tissue redder. At the same time it acts upon the heart also. The contraction of the heart has to overcome the resistance of the vessels, and to keep them full of blood. When the vessels dilate, they offer less resistance to the heart, and moreover, the whole mass of blood in them in the part is of necessity greater. To keep them full the heart must send more blood at a time in each pulse, or the pulses must more quickly follow one another.

But alcohol acts also on the heart itself, and makes it beat faster, and propel more blood in a given time.

Thus we see that the one early result of alcohol is to produce dilatation of the blood-vessels, both local and general, to quicken the action of the heart, and make it do more work in a given time. This latter action has been carefully studied by experiment. We may quote here the remarks of the late Dr. Parkes, who made many careful observations on this point. "Alcohol in healthy persons at first increases the force and quickness of the heart's action. In a healthy man I found that brandy augmented the rapidity of the pulse 13 per cent., and the force was also increased; taking the usual estimate of the heart's work, its daily excess of work with 4·8 fluid ounces of absolute alcohol was equal to 15·8 tons lifted one foot. With claret the results were almost identical." Dr. Parkes adds the important statement: "the period of rest of the heart was shortened, and its nutrition must therefore have been interfered with." But in smaller quantities it seems that the action of the heart may be increased, and yet its nutrition be maintained.

If this action on the heart and blood-vessels is only

temporary the effects are probably not permanent; but if kept up day after day, year after year, they lead to changes in the structure and action of the system, of which we shall speak later.

On the Nervous System.—Alcohol acts on the brain, the spinal cord, and the nerves when conveyed to them by the blood. It not only affects their function by producing quickened circulation through them, but it acts also upon their own proper structural elements. Its main action seems to be to lower the proper activity of the nervous matter. This is composed of cells and fibres; the former, which are chiefly in the brain and spinal cord, originate and receive nervous impulses; the latter convey them to and fro. Alcohol appears to have a special affinity for the substance composing these cells and fibres, and endowed with these peculiar nervous properties, and its effect is to diminish their activity, so that the cells originate and receive impulses more sluggishly, and the fibres conduct them less perfectly.*

* This, at least, is the view which our present knowledge indicates. According to some, the action of alcohol at first, or in moderate quantities, "is simply to augment the generation of nervous power. When this increased action of the nervous system is kept within certain limits the effect of the alcohol is beneficial; but when carried beyond a certain point the action is injurious and deteriorating, the spirit at length impairing and ultimately destroying the nutrition of

How is this effected? It used to be stated that alcohol was especially absorbed and retained by the brain substance, and could be found in combination with it in drinkers after it had been removed from the rest of the body; but this is now shown to be an error. But whether we suppose that it actually combines with the nervous matter, or only acts upon it by its presence as a sort of damper, we can have no doubt about its action. When we come to mention the effects of alcohol, as shown by the various mental and nervous symptoms which result from its misuse, we shall see a combination of the effects of vascular excitement and nervous weakening, and shall be able to trace a regular course in them. We shall find that at first there is for a time apparent overaction or excitement of the brain and nervous system, due, in part, to increased blood-supply and rapid circulation; in part, it may be, to direct stimulation of the nerve cells. Then as the effect is maintained or increased we shall see diminished activity. The higher functions of thought, will, and consciousness become impaired; the power of action, especially of controlled and balanced action, lessened; sense and feeling

---

the nervous matter" (Todd). But it is a question whether more force is generated or is only set free at first, the latter being the view now more commonly held.

are diminished; and, at last, unconsciousness and inaction results. We might trace all these out in detail, and see how the alcohol acting upon the brain in its various parts, upon the spinal marrow and upon the nerves, produces these varied effects, which all result from diminished action due to the presence of alcohol. If consciousness is the faculty of the part of the nervous system affected, this gives place first to lessened and then to lost consciousness; if feeling, it is first deadened, then lost; if motion, it is first irregular, then defective, then more or less entirely lost.

As a general rule, in man at any rate, these powers or functions of the nervous system are affected in a definite order, first the higher powers of the brain and then the spinal centres; but the extent to which they are affected varies in different cases, and as both are affected together, the continued action may show itself most clearly first on one or the other. That is to say, some men will continue pretty clear-headed even when their gait has become unsteady; whilst others will become drowsy or half unconscious before they show any marked want of equilibrium. In animals the case is rather different, and the effect of a large dose of alcohol on dogs is nearly always to produce at first paralysis of the hind legs, showing that the spinal cord towards its lower part is in them the first to give way.

The influence, not only of habit and constitution, but of disease or idiosyncracy, may also greatly determine the part of the nervous system which is chiefly affected. Great pain may keep up such a condition of excitement of the brain that the power of alcohol in producing unconsciousness is nearly lost. So, too, may mental excitement or emotion, or mental derangement; and it is from this cause that the great danger of alcohol to some persons arises. They can take a large quantity of alcohol for some time with little perceptible effect upon the brain. Then comes a time when the power of resistance is gone, and the brain suddenly gives way, delirium tremens, in some of the fiercest and strangest forms, resulting. So that this production of unconsciousness, which is so great a safeguard against dangerous results, cannot always be relied upon. We have seen cases of men who showed none of the ordinary signs of excess in drink, or at least so slight as to be almost imperceptible, or perhaps slightly tremulous and unable to walk, suddenly burst out into the most violent raving delirium with fury. In two such cases we have seen hospital patients who for two days had been in hospital and not taken any spirits, and had been admitted for indigestion with weakness in the legs, who were apparently perfectly rational and calm, go off suddenly into this violent frenzied delirium; and it was not till afterwards that the discovery was made that in both cases a long and deep debauch had immediately preceded the symptoms for which they sought admission to the hospital. Here the alcohol had been acting, but held in check; the deranged working of the nervous centres, produced by the opposing actions, resulted in the violent explosion of the pent-up forces.

Weakening, deranged action and paralysis of volition, sensation and motion, are thus seen to be the results of alcohol acting upon the nervous system.

These effects of alcohol on the circulatory and nervous systems are the most important for our present purpose, and they explain many of the other effects to which we cannot here allude, but which depend on disturbed action of various organs. Probably all tissues which have vital properties may be more or less affected by alcohol, and the changes connected with their nutrition and functions impaired; but the experiments hitherto made on these points are conflicting.

So also are the results as to the prevention of waste of the tissues, and the accumulation of fat, by the use of alcohol. Strong ground is afforded by what we see in the use of alcohol in disease for the belief that it has some such action, but how it acts we hardly know as yet; and such an action in health has been doubted, so that we will only mention this without discussing it.

It has been affirmed by some, and denied by others,

that alcohol lowers the temperature of the body. In moderate quantities it scarcely seems to affect it; in larger doses, it lowers it slightly in some cases; in poisonous doses the body is greatly cooled. We shall speak of this later.

What becomes of the alcohol taken into the body? Some have believed that it all enters into combination with the tissues, and after a time is all carried away out of the body by the natural channels. This is no doubt an error. Only a small portion gets out of the body as alcohol; the greater part, and nearly all if the quantity is not excessive, is used up—burnt, so to speak—in the body, and thus gives some small amount of nutriment. A very small quantity is carried off by the lungs and kidneys, unless a larger amount is taken than can be used up, when the excess is thus discharged.

We shall see presently that the fact that alcohol is eliminated by the kidneys is important as explaining its special effect in producing disease of those organs; just as the passage of all the alcohol from the stomach through the liver explains the frequent disease of the latter organ in drinkers.

We cannot go further into detail upon this subject; indeed, there is yet much obscurity upon the action of alcohol in the system. We have said enough to serve as a guide to what we have to say as to its use.

CHAPTER III.

THE EFFECTS OF ALCOHOL WHEN TAKEN IN EXCESS.

WE have seen that the first tangible result of taking any form of alcoholic beverage, so far as it reveals itself to our consciousness, is a slight stimulant effect. A glow of warmth is diffused over the body; there is a sensation of pleasure, which takes its special colour from the surroundings of the moment, showing itself in relief from discomfort, whether mental or physical, in increased enjoyment of the flow of conversation, in a freer current of thought and social intercourse, or any of the other subtle harmonies of life. It may be objected that such is not always the effect; that it is largely modified by habit, by the condition of digestion, the drink taken, and the special temperament and constitution of the individual; and we fully admit this objection. But, allowing for all such differences in degree, such is the most common sensible effect of the "wine which maketh glad the heart of man."

But if more than a certain quantity is taken, further results rapidly ensue. The point of stimulation only may be reached by a continuance of repeated small doses; as, for example, in a long after-dinner talk, only just enough being taken to keep up this stage: but it is easy to go beyond this point, when other effects appear.

Thought no longer only flows more freely and conversation more pleasantly; there is some loss of control of thought, the ideas fleet rapidly, but are not steadily retained, the too rapid stream overflows its banks, and is broken into eddies and currents in its course, so that there arise confusion of thought, want of clearness of apprehension, and inability to reason soundly and consecutively. Nor is the intellect alone perturbed; the emotions are less under control: mirth gives way to hilarity, and this to boisterous merriment, which may subside into the opposite of sullenness, or go on to wild excitement; moral control is lost, and the actions are the result of fitful caprice, or the outcome of baser passions. The voluntary and involuntary motions of the body show a like want of control; the more delicate movements, those which require long-trained and adjusted co-operation of nerve centres and groups of muscles, cannot be performed; even those which are so far habitual and automatic that we can perform them without conscious effort, and may even do them during sleep, become difficult or are done imperfectly. It is well known that many actions, such as walking, are done almost without volition when the power has been acquired, so that we only will to go to such-and-such a place, or to walk about, and our attention, so long as all goes well, is no longer needful. We balance the body, throw out one foot, poise ourselves on the other, plant the foot, and so on, without the least consciousness that we are doing so; though, should any accident derange some part of the mechanism, we are painfully alive to the various movements. Other habitual actions require a greater control and attention, yet may become almost equally automatic as walking. There are many men who write constantly or much, who become equally facile; there is to them no conscious pause or thought between the volition to write, and the appearance of the word on the paper; and so established is the connexion of thought and word, that for each idea there is a sign which they place upon paper, and the sign may be one which they have adopted for brevity of expression, but which they use as their token for the thought or word quite unconsciously, and require great effort not to use. We might thus instance also other acquired movements, such as playing musical instruments, knitting, and working various machines, which by habit become capable of execution almost unconsciously. It is these movements which first show that disorder which results from loss of control. There may be perfect consciousness of the right method of doing them, and an endeavour to do them, but they are less delicately combined, need greater effort for their performance, and when a certain point of intoxication has been reached, they are either impossible if very complex, or are done clumsily and irregularly. It is thus the movements which are acquired with most pains, such as writing and mechanical movements, which are first disordered; then those which, though complex, like walking, are not the outcome of great training and effort, yet require regularly co-ordinated action for their performance. On a rather different level we may place the act of speech, one of the most thoroughly acquired yet most complex of our actions. It would be interesting to study in detail the mode in which this is affected, and to show how the derangements of the several groups of nervous centres cause a variety of changes in its performance. We must only just mention them in passing. To speak a word, we must first in some way have the idea of the word in the mind, or rather a word-idea is our mental cheque or telegraph-form for the word. This word-idea must pass to the nerve-centre which controls the expression, from which again all the orders, or stimuli, to the centres which control each part of the speaking of the word must pass; and these orders, in the transmission, must be harmonised so that they may produce not merely the sounds needed, but the sounds in their due order, force, and inflection. There are required for each word which we speak, special movements of the tongue, mouth, palate, and throat, organised and united into one, and all controlled by separate and numerous centres, and the defective adjustment of any one of these deranges and spoils the speaking of the word. But in speech it is not one word, but a continuous flow of words that we employ, all separate, yet all harmonised and succeeding each other with a rapidity which seems to leave no time for special arranging of the organs. When, therefore, control is less active, the reins slackened so to speak, words may be wrongly spoken through the wrong word-idea being chosen; or they may be omitted, or curtailed, or misplaced; or they may be imperfectly made up, lacking some parts, or jumbled together in confused expression; and the disorder of the uttering organs of speech may cause them to be clipt at the ends, stammered, or mouthed, or " thick " from defective action of the tongue. Thus we might see how the loss of control of idea at the one terminal, causes confusion of thought and wrong choice of words, and at the other, how the organs of expression fail from maladaptation, and we might try to show how all the degrees of speech-affection are indices of stages of intoxication.

In a yet further stage of intoxication, we find that movements which are naturally combined in harmony, and which we cannot derange without voluntary effort, become deranged; this especially in the case of actions which, like those of the eyes, are symmetrical for two corresponding organs. In healthy eyes, the muscles which move the eyeballs, so as to direct them towards any given object, or to concentrate them upon a nearer or further point, act automatically, so that the images in the two retinæ fall on corresponding points, and are organised into one image in the brain. When, from injury or disease, one of the muscles is but slightly deranged, or when we squint voluntarily, the image in one eye falls upon a point in the retina which does not correspond with that of the other image, and thus two images are seen.* Now this derangement occurs under the influence of drinking—the eyes do not move in harmony, hence the man "sees double." (We do not mean to say that this is the only way in which intoxication causes double vision, for others may and do occur, and two images and more may be seen with one eye; but to understand the mechanism of these, a much more elaborate account of the structure and actions of the eye would be needed.)

We may here pause to note that the rapidity with which these effects are produced, as well as their character, varies immensely with the person, with the kind of drink, the rate at which it is taken, and many other circumstances. Moreover, many of them may be absent,

---

* For further details on this interesting subject see the work in this series on 'The Eye.'

and the process may cease at any point if the drinking be suspended.

Before going further, we may inquire what is the mode of action of alcohol by which these results are produced. We have spoken of excitement, followed by confusion of intellect, emotion and action; and we shall see that a yet further stage may be reached in which all the powers are in abeyance and dormant, and a living death, or mere vegetative life, remains. But all these may be summed up in the words, loss of control. The higher intellectual centres cease to control the thought, the moral control is lost over the emotions, the centres which govern and direct combined action no longer guide the lower and subordinate ones, and they in turn hold less in check and tone the muscles and their nerves. It would be easy to show that it is not only the higher powers which are affected, that the lower centres, too, are directly acted upon. And as we have already seen in speaking of the physiological action of alcohol, the earliest glow of warmth, flush of face, and quickened beat of heart, are alike due to a check of control, so that the minute blood-vessels dilate owing to loss of moderating force.

For the present we need not carry into further detail the picture of the state of the drunken, with which we are all too familiar, as it appears to outward observation; and the drunkard has himself no farther consciousness when he has reached the stage which we have indicated, so that he cannot tell what he feels or experiences. We have touched upon this state in speaking of physiological action. "The worst estate of man is that wherein he loses the knowledge and government of himself."

If we wrote only for those who, whether rarely or often, drink to such excess as this, we should waste our labour, for no such advice as we could give, grounded on general considerations of health, would serve to deter them from indulging their habits. We might paint ruin staring them in the face—ruin of body, mind, and soul, or ply them with exhortations to virtue and temperance; but to show them their state from a scientific point of view, would be like putting a tissue-paper barrier to stop a waterfall, the fragments would soon dance in the eddies.

But it is a melancholy fact that a very large number of those who are permanently injured by drinking are of those who rarely or never drink beyond the stage of slight excitement, or even halt before that point. For one man who is injured by being drunk often, there are twenty or more who are more seriously injured by drinking and never approaching the verge of intoxication. A man may drink in such a way as never to feel consciously excited or embarrassed, yet ruin his health, and cut short his days more speedily and surely than the man who is dead-drunk every Saturday night.

We may here add a little to what we have already said on physiological action, action, that is to say, on the working of the system.

Every time a machine is set a-going it consumes material which sets it at work, whether coal or gas; it does some work, if only in wasted movement, and it wears itself out a little. It has waste products in the shape of ashes from the coal or coke, and it may be also of the material on which it acts, and if it wear itself rapidly, as a grindstone, for instance, there will be the products of its wear. With one most important qualification the human body may be likened to a machine, for it is constantly at work; its boilers need replenishing, its stokehole filling; it has waste products both of the fuel and of its own wear; it does work of all sorts, and tends to wear out. The difference is that the machine itself is a living machine and constantly repairs and renews itself, though at last its power of self-repair fails, and it falls into decay.

Now it is easy to see that, by putting certain fuel into a machine, we may do several things. The fuel may make too hot a fire, and so over-heat the boilers, dry up the oil of the bearings, crack the metal, spoil the varnish, or make the machine go at a dangerous speed. Or it may be corrosive, and erode and spoil the furnace and boilers, and perhaps other parts. Or if the machine be a self-repairing one, it may be hindered from proper repair, whether by want of due supply, want of time, or spoiling of the several parts.

Alcohol may act in all these ways when taken in excess, or in an improper manner, and the results are seen in the various diseases which result from its use. Even to mention all these diseases by name would require too much space, nor, without a description of all the organs, could we give any adequate idea of them. The most useful plan, we think, will be to classify them under three or four heads; to describe so much of the more common as will be of practical use, and to mention only some of the rest, which come under the more special knowledge of the doctor, as follows:—

I. Comparatively slight disorders due to use of excess of alcohol, or its use at improper times.

II. The effects of large repeated doses in producing simple intoxication, or the peculiar forms of alcohol poisoning known as *delirium tremens*, &c.

III. Diseases resulting from the continued use of alcohol.
    1. General deterioration.
    2. Destruction of special organs of the body.

I. *Slight disorders due to excessive or improper use.*—Returning to our machine, we see that if we use the wrong fuel even once, we may choke the flues, corrode the pipes, and so on, and leave a certain result which will last only for a time, if we have it repaired, and cease to use the fuel. If we use it again and again, we shall run the greater risk of damaging our machine irreparably, so that it will always go a little wrong or shakily, though it may go for a long time; or it may be so damaged as to break down altogether.

So we see that wine or spirits, taken at wrong times or in excess, cause disordered digestion, constipation, general malaise, inability to work, nervousness, shakiness of the hands, and so on, with no greater result if discontinued; that if taken once or repeatedly in large quantities, it may cause drunkenness or *delirium tremens;* that if taken for months or years in any excess, however slight, it may cause degeneration or destruction, for all practical purposes, of certain parts of the body, or a deterioration of the whole. It is mainly the slighter forms that we have now to consider.

Alcoholic Indigestion.—One of the commonest, least recognised, and most insidious results of slight excess is the derangement of digestion known as "*alcoholic dyspepsia.*" A multitude of well-to-do and respectable people suffer from it without either knowing its cause, or being aware that it is preventible, and it is one of the commonest and most troublesome of the complaints which bring patients to the "out-patient" rooms of our hospitals (especially "chest" hospitals). The symptoms vary, but when slight are something like these: A man (or woman either) complains of slight loss of appetite, especially in the morning for breakfast; feels languid either on rising or early in the day; retches a little in the morning, and perhaps brings up a little phlegm only, or may actually vomit; or may be able to take breakfast, but feels sick after it. Towards the middle of the morning he is heavy and languid, perhaps, and does not feel easy till he has had a glass of sherry or some spirits, then gets on pretty well, and can eat lunch or dinner. Or if worse, the appetite for both is defective, and there is undue weight and discomfort after meals; and with this there is often some slight soreness of the throat, tickling sensations, and tendency to a little cough, especially in the morning. Not uncommonly there is also a tendency to constipation, and a feeling of discomfort and weight in the right side.

Now all these symptoms *may* be due to other causes; but when taken together—and especially when the loss of appetite for breakfast is most marked—they are by far most commonly due to alcohol, taken in excess or at wrong times. They are, of course, worst in those who drink in large excess, and there is often then a tremulous condition of the hands and tongue, and other disorders. But many people get into this state, either occasionally or habitually, by taking a glass or two of wine or spirits on an empty stomach late at night; and during the day; whilst taking their ordinary stimulant at meal-times, indulging also in a glass or two of sherry in the middle of the morning, and perhaps, too, at other times. And we must emphasise the statement that such effects are often seen in persons who are abstemious through the day, and moderate at dinner, but who take wine or spirits before going to bed, in order to rid them of mental excitement and enable them to sleep. So slight are the other general effects, that were it not that this condition has a dangerous tendency to cause fresh recourse to drink for its temporary relief, and that there can be no doubt that, in the long-run, the constant recurrence of slight poisoning tends to set up organic disease, we might say less about this result of alcohol.

Amongst the labouring classes, and in certain trades, especially those involving long hours and night-work, as well as in many of the more educated classes, spirits are especially taken; and when taken undiluted or with a little water, are especially liable to cause these symptoms. And this is one of the reasons why the "morning nip" before breakfast, or before work, is so often indulged in and is so dangerous; for while it relieves for a time the tremor and the discomfort, it only aggravates the condition which produces them.

Trembling.—Another condition which we have just

mentioned, one of the special results of alcohol, is *tremor*, shakiness of the hands, so that they are unsteady when at rest, or if the hand is held out it is seen to vibrate slightly; or in the more advanced condition, "shakes like an aspen leaf." We have seen this in a spirit-drinker as almost the only symptom; he was a barber, working early and late in shaving, and to "steady his hand" took constantly raw spirits, at first to relieve fatigue, then because he found that if he discontinued, his hand was too shaky to use the razor. Complete abstinence from alcohol, and strong coffee, quite removed his tremors and his desire for spirits. And this is only a sample of a class, though few, it may be feared, have so much self-control as to relinquish the habit, or so honest a purpose in drinking. This tremor has its highest expression during the condition of mental derangement known as *delirium tremens*. We need not dwell upon the other slight effects mentioned above.

II. The effects of large repeated doses in causing drunkenness and, later, *delirium tremens*.—It would be outside our purpose to speak much of these. We have just described some of the stages of intoxication, and others will appear from the description of the physiological action of alcohol. The evils of drunkenness are so obvious to all in their social, moral, and physical aspects, and so wide a field of discussion would be opened, that we may leave this for others; we have already said that it is a great mistake to believe that those who never become intoxicated do not injure themselves and others by drinking.

The condition known as *delirium tremens* may be, and perhaps most frequently is, produced without actual drunkenness in the common use of the word. Those who drink hard but keep from actual loss of consciousness, especially those engaged in hard mental work, or subjected to great moral strain or shock; and, too, those of certain temperaments, are peculiarly liable to it. It is preceded usually by loss of sleep, ideas of persecution or of injury with no foundation in fact, and slight hallucinations, especially at night, the man the while in the day looking anxious, slightly excited, nervous and tremulous, and perhaps narrating, as actual occurrences, the hallucinations of the preceding night. Then the senses are partly lost, he sees spectres, horrible and foul creatures about him, has all sorts of painful terrifying visions (whence the common name of "the horrors"), is extremely tremulous, and either excited or lies prostrate, trembling violently on movement, sleepless, anxious, and a prey to spectres and terrors of the imagination. But we need follow him no further to recovery or death, but leave the study of his condition to the doctor and the moralist.

Another condition often and wrongly confounded with

this is that known as *dipsomania*. It has in common with it the fact that those who are a prey to it do get delirium tremens by their drinking; but it is a name properly applied only to a disease, usually associated with mental disease or inherited tendency, in which there occurs, periodically, an irresistible craving for drink, not always limited to alcoholic drinks; and during the continuance of this craving everything is drunk which can be got hold of. The attack over, whether by intoxication or by restraint, the patient (for such he should be) is free for a time, often a long time, from any tendency to drink. This is, and should be, regarded and treated as a mental disease, and has no resemblance to the commoner forms of excess in drinking. But we must add that drinking itself induces a strong craving for alcohol, so that sometimes it may be hard to say whether a man is only suffering from his bad habits or from a mental disease. The chief point of difference is that in the true dipsomaniac the attacks are periodical, and there is often a family tendency to insanity or to other nervous diseases.

III. The diseases which result from the continued excess in alcohol are very numerous, often combined in the same person, and, as is the case with nearly all diseases of one part, leading to further changes in other parts.

1. We may speak first of *general* conditions, affecting all

parts of the body. And here we cannot even attempt to mention all those slighter general states which are so commonly seen in those who drink. The moral tone is lowered, there is often a coarseness of look and manner which mark the general deterioration; the memory is less clear and retentive, the grasp of the intellect is enfeebled, there is less power of mental work, and loss of that self-control and self-respect which gain the confidence of others. Often there is a peculiar suspicion shown in the look, a suspicion of being suspected; or a restless wandering look which betrays to the careful observer a consciousness of deterioration. Then the face assumes a slightly puffy look, due at first to want of "tone" of the muscles of expression, and later to actual degeneration, and to the accumulation of fat over them. Or, in rarer instances, there is instead a pinched, wasted look, conjoined with a similar condition of the body.

The most common *general* condition is that which is known as "fatty degeneration," which consists of two quite distinct parts. All over the body, beneath the skin, where it is thicker in some parts than others, and also in all the chinks and spaces around and between the chief organs (except the brain and spinal cord), there is in the healthy state what is known as fatty or adipose tissue, which is made up of minute cells filled with oil, closely packed together. In addition to this, some organs, especially the liver, contain some oil, which is burnt as fuel when needed, as we see in hybernating animals, who are said to store up a large quantity before the winter. The use of the fat or oil is to form, as it were, pads, and to lubricate the muscles, to keep in the warmth, and to be burnt up or used up when wanted. One common effect of alcohol is to cause an increase of this fat, so that in some cases it becomes very excessive, especially in the liver and in other internal parts where only a small quantity ought to be present.

Another change, much more serious and important, but which goes by the same name, is a change of other tissues into fat. All the important organs of the body are composed of various forms of "albuminoid" matter, and are of "protoplasmic" nature; that is, they are highly complex organic bodies, having some relation to albumen, and endowed with living powers, which vary with the different tissues they constitute. Thus we have muscle, made up of minute filaments which have the power of contracting; nerves, formed by delicate cords, which convey nerve-impulses of whatever nature; cells, some of which make ferments, &c., to digest food, some prepare it for use, and so on, but all go to make up what we call organs, and have special work of some kind, and a peculiar power of doing it. Now when one of these elements dies or slowly decays, the albuminous or protoplasmic substance of which it is made first loses its peculiar vital properties, then breaks up into minute granules, and these granules are further altered till they become oil globules, in which state they are carried off by the blood to be burnt up. We cannot follow all the steps of the process chemically, but we know that the protoplasm loses its nitrogen, oil containing none, and when the stage of oil drops is reached, we know that the part of the organism is for all work and use dead.

It is this form of "fatty degeneration" which alcohol especially produces and which makes its results so dangerous. We see it most in the heart and liver, but an analogous process occurs in the blood-vessels, in the nerves, and indeed in all vital organs. It means simply living decay of parts of our most important organs, piecemeal death going on in the live body. And when alcohol is taken in large repeated doses continuously, this change may become very advanced in but a short time. Other poisons produce it more rapidly, especially phosphorus.

There is another general deterioration, which is of almost equal importance. All organs contain a material which forms their skeleton or framework, holds the more special vital parts together, and forms coverings for them. This is called "connective" or fibrous tissue.

Now this, when in proper quantity and arrangement, is essential, but when it grows beyond normal limits it displaces and destroys the more important vital elements, so that its overgrowth in any organ causes to an equal degree undergrowth or destruction of those more important parts. Nor is this all; for this tissue grows from cells which are soft and elastic, but gradually these are joined together into fibres, and these into thicker fibres, and as they grow and get stronger and denser, they contract and get shorter, so that they crush the softer and more yielding tissues which they surround and divide. Now a scaffolding or framework is very useful in proper limits; but if we use growing trees and their branches for our timbers and joists, and they can, and do, still grow and flourish, our house will not be likely to be very permanent; nor does this simile give more than a very feeble idea of what happens in the case of a contracting tissue in an organ.

It is from this overgrowth or fibrous change that many of the most serious internal diseases result; and it produces especially the diseases of the liver and kidneys which are so fatal to chronic drinkers.

But there are other general constitutional conditions which are produced by over-indulgence in drinking, even when the habit is never carried to excess of visible amount. It is far more difficult to classify and accurately describe these general states of the system. They probably depend on an early stage of functional derangement, caused by the organic diseases of which we are about to speak, before they have reached any perceptible degree. A tendency to gout, some forms of rheumatism, stone and the like, are now very commonly believed to result from habitual slight excess in alcohol. Very strong opinions to this effect have of late years been expressed by some eminent surgeons and physicians whose large experience in these particular diseases entitles their opinion to respect. But we must not forget that it is not merely the direct effect of alcohol itself with which we have to do—over-indulgence in wine or beer means, commonly, excess in eating, bad habits as to rest, exercise, and air, and many other evil habits which combine to produce the results mentioned. They are, however, indirectly attributable to the use of alcohol.

2. The destruction of particular organs is rather in the province of the physician than suited to a popular essay. The whole system may be involved, or only certain organs, especially the heart, stomach, liver, kidneys, and brain; but there is also a peculiar tendency to some chronic forms of lung-disease, and to fatal results in accidental diseases, such as erysipelas, inflammation of the lungs, &c. The organ affected, and the form of disease, depend in part upon the form of alcohol and its degree of dilu

tion, upon the idiosyncracy of the person, and upon his general temperament and habits.

The *stomach* may be damaged by the direct action of strong alcohol, by repeated derangement, or by changes like those of other organs. We have seen that one of the effects of alcohol, especially in the form of wine or spirits, is at first to stimulate the secretion of the stomach, and possibly also the movements on which the digestion partly depends. We found, too, that the local effect is to dilate the blood-vessels. This over-action when excessive or needless is followed by a perturbed condition, partly due to an exhaustion from the over-action, partly to the direct damaging effect of the alcohol; and the derangement of the liver adds also to the disturbance. Now when this irritation is repeated day by day, week by week, and year by year, we need not be surprised that the stomach gets altered in its structure, even if the temporary derangement is only slight at any given time. *Gutta cavat lapidem*, and a " drop too much " is not needed to wear out the stomach. But although we do find various diseases in the stomach, and see the effects of deranged digestion as a result of drinking, there is a marvellous power both of resistance and recovery on the part of the stomach, so that some long-standing topers maintain their digestion and have healthy stomachs to the last. The evil is bad enough, we need not exaggerate it by the absurd and impossible pictures of the stomach with which teetotal lecturers delight to terrify their credulous audiences.

The worst form of stomach disease occurs in those who take spirits on an empty stomach, and particularly in the morning with "bitters," "absinthe," and the like, which also help to irritate the stomach coats.

The *liver* is peculiarly liable to disease, for all, or nearly all, the alcohol taken into the stomach goes into the blood-vessels which lead to the liver, and all the blood from the stomach circulates through the minute blood-vessels of the liver before it goes on to the heart. Hence the evil effects of which we have spoken are usually most strongly marked in the liver.

The changes in the *heart* are especially due to over-excitement and consequent hypertrophy, combined with the slow deterioration or fatty degeneration of its muscle-fibres, and accumulation of fat on its surface also. And other more complex derangements also occur.

The *kidneys* receive from the blood all the materials of tissue destruction or waste which are not burnt off the lungs or excreted by the skin, as well as the greater part of excess of water in the blood. Alcohol has a peculiar property of exciting the kidneys to over-action by temporary dilatation of the blood-vessels, which produce a condition like that seen on the skin in blushing. It probably also acts as an irritant on the glandular cells of the organ, causing them, if only slightly stimulated, to excrete more organic material than before. Hence the first and direct action is irritation, slight and transient, but capable of repetition.

But a part of the action is more complex, and is probably due to the effects upon other tissues and on the blood. We have said that the kidneys excrete or remove from the body the waste products of tissue-combustion, and waste, and many other bodies, such as salts of various kinds which only get into the blood by accident or design, and stay only a short time in the body. But before the waste tissue products are removed by the kidneys, they are usually in great part converted into the form of a salt called urea, which is readily soluble in water. It is now believed by many physiologists that the liver plays a great part in this transformation; and it is also at least known that retarded oxidation of tissue waste prevents the proper reduction into urea. Now, by whatever mechanism, whether by its action on the liver, or on the blood, or by its power of retarding oxidation, alcohol does prevent in some degree the proper changes in the tissue waste, so that a larger part of it than usual passes out in the form of uric acid, urates and other substances, which are less soluble, more irritant, and defectively oxidized.

And whether from this cause, or from repeated congestion and irritation, alcohol leads at last to widespread disease of the kidneys in a large number of cases; in most to the fibrous form of degeneration; but in a few more rapidly to other forms.

We have already pointed out that the *nervous system*, in which term are included not only the nervous centres, such as the brain and spinal cord, but also all the ganglia, nerve fibres, and their terminations, undergo various changes as the result of drinking, and that these changes, whether transient or permanent, show themselves by altered function and by diminished or deranged power. The study of all these conditions would be a too technical and too prolonged one for its introduction here, we must therefore leave it, mentioning only some of the more obvious results.

The very important question of the effect of drinking in causing the loss of mental power must detain us a moment. Many would ascribe moral deterioration also to an organic change in the brain, but we cannot fully agree with this view. Moral character is very largely influenced by habit, by the acquired control of the highest cerebral centres over the lower; and hence the continual paralysis of that control, and the constant abolition of all power of self-restraint must, of course, aid largely in moral deterioration. But we cannot go further than this, the habitual drunkard is morally defective from the outset, and his habits give full play to the action of all the baser tendencies of his nature. Drunkenness is more a vice than a disease.

But does the constant use of alcohol in moderate or not greatly excessive quantity cause moral deterioration? No more important question could be proposed than this, nor easily one more difficult of answer. We believe the true reply to be that whatever quantity causes any temporary loss of moral control does, if repeated, lead to moral deterioration, but that short of this no such result is produced. But we must say that of those who habitually use alcohol, even in what is regarded as moderation, a very large number do from time to time exceed the limit of safety, and weaken moral control.

The effect of the use of alcohol on the mental powers, observation, memory, and judgment, &c., is exceedingly variable. There are some whose nervous system is especially prone to be affected by alcohol; others who resist its action, even in large doses, for a very long time. The results of habitual excess are seen in many cases in a decline of intellectual power, loss of memory, &c., but this chiefly when there is great excess with defective power of resistance. We are speaking now only of the permanent effects. No one can doubt the constant effect so long as alcohol is being taken in excess. And we have no doubt that a large part of the mental deterioration which we see in chronic drinkers is simply the resultant of long-continued want of exercise of the mental powers, which for their proper action require continued exercise and habit. Beyond this, there is actual decay of nerve tissue, partly from disuse, partly the consequent of changes of nutritive action and of vascular supply.

We are here again met with the inquiry whether the habitual use of alcohol in anything short of excess causes diminution of mental power. And we must again reply that we know of no evidence that any such diminution is produced, so long as there is no *excess*, in the proper meaning of the term, but that there is great chance of reduction of mental power with far less than is commonly regarded as excess. And even when there is no permanent injury, however slight, the amount of mental work which can be done without the effect is certainly diminished by very slight excess. On the other hand, we shall show that a moderate use of alcohol is in many cases a safeguard against the over-exertion of the mind to the injury of the brain.

Of other permanent nerve disorders caused by alcohol we need say little here. The various forms of paralysis, convulsions, and mental derangement as the result of great excess, form a very important study for the physician, but never result from any slight degree of drinking, and are beyond our province here. The researches of late years have shown that excess in alcohol can and does produce nervous disorders which very closely resemble those due to organic disease; the important practical point for those who are not doctors is never to supply stimulants to persons with paralysis and the like without the doctor's orders. We have known two patients killed in this way, by secretly supplying them with spirits; they were suffering from paralysis actually caused by alcohol, and their friends thought they had serious disease, and wanted "keeping up," to which they had been used; the doctor's orders of strict abstinence were regarded as his "fad," and the patients were "kept up" into fatal delirium tremens.

We see, then, that intemperance is a most fruitful cause of disease; and this is true not only of the individual, but of the population taken as a whole. For not more surely does decay and degeneration of the body of the individual occur, as the result of excessive drinking, than an injury to the body corporate; for the disease is propagated in the offspring, and tells upon the community. The children of parents addicted to drink, even if not decrepit and deformed, have the tendency to degeneration in some one or other way implanted in their constitution, and like a birth-mark, or a mole, or the colour of hair and eyes, it may be handed down to posterity. There is no more wonderful problem in nature than this handing down of tendencies, and even instincts and emotions, from parents to children. Account for it as we may, we must accept the fact that acquired tendencies to disease are so propagated, and that especially the children of parents whose brains are injured by alcohol are more prone than others to mental disease, and to those widely varied diseases which we call "nervous." We might enlarge much upon this branch of our subject, and trace out the effects of physical, mental, and moral deterioration of parents upon their offspring; but this has already been frequently done by others. There is good reason to believe that a propensity to drinking is often hereditary, that propensity having been in the first instance acquired. But it must be remembered that we speak here of the results of excess, and not of moderation and temperance.

In concluding this part of our subject we must say a word or two upon the treatment of excess in alcohol. The value of restraint and seclusion, and the ways in which they should be enforced, we cannot here discuss. But many men who desire to give up drinking find it hard to do so. One great necessity is the substitution of something to replace the alcohol. Bitter aromatic tonics best serve this purpose, and may be taken at the times when spirits and water would otherwise be drunk. Those who have acquired the habit of taking wine or spirits at night or in the morning, will often find that a glass of milk will serve their purpose better. In all confirmed cases total abstinence and medical treatment are advisable.

CHAPTER IV.

THE USES OF ALCOHOL AND ALCOHOLIC BEVERAGES.

ALCOHOLIC drinks have their uses in health and in disease: we may consider the former first. It may be laid down as an axiom that a man of good constitution and in good health, with healthy surroundings of food, air, and exercise, requires no alcohol. But so numerous are the departures from the typical standard of health and of good health conditions that a need of alcohol sometimes arises.

Age exerts an important influence. Children under 10 years of age ought never to take alcohol unless during illness or under medical advice; and in the large majority of cases, more harm than good is done by taking wine or beer between the ages of 14 and 25, especially at the period of adolescence.* But between the age of 9 or 10,

* "Plato forbids children wine till eighteen years of age, and being drunk till forty."—Montaigne.

and 14 or 15, there is often a rapid growth and a great strain both on the mental and physical capacities, and if this cannot be met by abundant rest, exercise, air, and food, there is often good from a moderate allowance of alcohol. But in this, as in other matters of the kind, there is great variety in the age at which it is needed, and the amount required. From 25 to 35 or 40, if there is good health, alcohol is certainly not needed, provided always that the surroundings be healthy. And it is especially between 20 and 30 that the use of alcohol habitually in any excess has the most deleterious influence both upon body and mind. After 35 or 40 the uses of alcohol, in moderation, are most perceptible, and from 40 to 60 it is most needed. Later, many who have been in the habit of using wine or spirits, find it necessary to restrict the quantity, and to take it in a different form.

But after all, such rules as these are subject to great modification in individual cases, and hence are of little value in practice; and it will be well to inquire what alcohol can do to promote health, and in what ways it may be usefully employed.

Alcohol has been supposed to aid digestion, and itself also to act as a food; to promote nutrition; to be a stimulant and a sedative, and to give warmth to the body. We may inquire how far it really possesses these qualities, and to what degree they may be utilised: they are so much involved in each other that we cannot absolutely separate them.

On Digestion.—Whether alcohol is a food or not it unquestionably aids in the digestion and assimilation of food in some cases, where without it food is not properly digested. We will not now discuss the various theories of its action. It may be, by its action directly on the stomach, promoting the flow of blood; by permitting of that rest of nervous energy which is one of the main aids to healthy digestion; by increasing secretion, or what not—all of which might be amply discussed in a work on medicine; but the fact remains that, in a large number of cases, a moderate allowance of alcohol taken with food does aid digestion and thus promote nutrition. Even in infancy, in some states of wasting, alcohol is of great value. Wine is the form in which the alcohol is most often useful for this purpose. In rapidly growing and unhealthy children, who take their food badly, and are not nourished by it—indeed in many conditions of continued ill-health in childhood and early youth—a small daily allowance of wine, port or sherry, diluted with water and taken at meals, is extremely beneficial.

In early manhood and womanhood, if the habits are properly regulated, there is more rarely the actual necessity for stimulants to aid digestion. More often their discontinuance would restore it. Young women, especially of sedentary habits and keeping late hours, or neglecting to take exercise, with no special duties requiring thought and energy, very often suffer from capricious appetite, some symptoms of indigestion, languor, and debility, for which they are often advised to take, or do take, wine, both at and between meals, and in the multitude of instances only keep up and aggravate the very symptoms of which they complain. And we might say the same of many others—especially young men who take wine or beer in the morning or at mid-day, or who fast all day, and are exhausted and void of appetite at dinner-time. Alcohol is not here the remedy; light food at mid-day, with chocolate or milk, and, if need be, a cup of tea or coffee an hour before dinner, are far better treatment. In a great number of cases, proper food taken at proper times would make the use of alcohol for this purpose unnecessary.

A very large number of middle-aged and elderly people do, however, find that some wine or beer at dinner aids them in digestion. We might provide them with a number of theories as to the way in which this occurs; we prefer to point out the fact, and to caution them against converting a right use into a misuse. Nor must the effect of habit in creating necessities be forgotten.

We may here say a word for one mode of action of alcohol which is too often left out of sight by strictly scientific people. Emotions, such as pleasure, happiness, discontent, and the like, are too evanescent and imponderable quantities to gain the notice of the physiologist and chemist. It is true that the modern vitalist looks upon them as an indication of the state of the brain-cells which may be of interest and value, but the truly scientific man is too much engrossed with physical properties to care for the existence of such mere feelings in other people. He can see that alcohol causes the blood-vessels to dilate, the gastric follicles to secrete; that in excess it flushes the face, makes the gait unsteady, and so on, and condemn this action as needless and wasteful. But the effect even of slight and almost unconscious states of feeling upon all these processes seem to escape his notice. The sight of green trees, the sound of the sea, the smell of flowers, may give energy and appetite to the invalid in such a way as to be perceptible. The healthy man may be less conscious of such emotion, but it may strongly influence him. Appetite and digestion, and many other functions, are very greatly under the control of feeling. Some cannot eat heartily in company, nor others alone; a smell, a slight taste, will destroy the appetite and digestion. Perhaps more than anything else, great mental preoccupation, such as business cares and worries, may completely check digestion. Now alcohol in some of the liquors which contain but a very small quantity, such as light ales or wines (we would especially mention light dry effervescing wines), and even a small amount of these, do check in many cases the current of these thoughts and cares for a time, and the slight degree of pleasure thus excited serves to set the digestive process in action. This is not only a lawful use of alcohol, it is one which is in many cases very beneficial, and to neglect it would be wrong. Because ninety-nine persons out of a hundred misuse it, it none the less remains true that it has a right use. Let no one, however, mistake our meaning. Strong wine is not nearly so well calculated to produce this effect as light wine diluted with water, and where a light heart and cheerful company make this needless, it is an abuse of alcohol to take it.

To speak of the danger of producing such slight excitement of the heart's action as this, to regard it as shortening the life and producing physical and mental decay, is an abuse of science; if it were true, every exertion, every pleasing emotion, nay, all activity of every sort, would tend to shorten our days, and they alone would be wise and happy who existed in torpor, with only such food as they could get with the least possible exertion, and that only sufficient to keep body and soul together. Science will never gain a proper influence over the actions of intelligent men so long as her assertions are contrary to the common-sense and intelligence of rational beings.

Alcohol as a *Food*.—The question whether alcohol is a food is one which has been obscured by numerous misstatements and fallacies. It has been discussed on chemical and physiological grounds, and by the light of experience. Chemically, it is a fact that alcohol contains no nitrogen; the body requires nitrogen for its nutrition, hence it is stated that alcohol cannot support life alone. But this is also true of starch and oil, two of our chief food ingredients. If alcohol is burnt up in the body it does act to some extent as a food. Some physiologists have stated that all the alcohol taken passes out of the body again unchanged. This, if true, would show that it is not a food; but further experiments have shown that only a very small quantity of the alcohol does pass out unaltered, the greater part is burnt up in the body. Certain observations on persons in old age or disease show that life can be supported for a long time on a diet which contains little but pure spirits and water; in these exceptional cases the alcohol evidently acting as a food.

But all these results of experiment and observation only refer to very exceptional conditions, and are not of much value for our purpose. For no one would think of taking, as a food, in health, an amount of alcohol sufficient to be an important ingredient in his diet. Four glasses of sherry would supply at the outside only an infinitesimal part of the carbon daily needed by a healthy man, that is to say, from the alcohol itself. It is scarcely necessary, then, to consider this question; it is one of little practical moment.

The more important question is, if an allowance of alcohol is taken with food of ordinary kinds, is more work done in the system than if no alcohol is taken. Many experiments have been made to decide this. Like all such experiments they are very difficult to conduct accurately; and the quantity of alcohol given has exceeded that which could be called moderate. According to the late Dr. Parkes, one of the greatest authorities on the subject, the effect on bodily labour is that a small quantity of alcohol does not produce much effect, but that more than two fluid ounces daily manifestly lessens the power of sustained and strong muscular work. Even when the quantity is not excessive it seems doubtful whether alcohol is beneficial, for it increases the action of the heart beyond the necessary degree; hence it should only be used when an excessive effort is to be made, which must be made without giving the heart proper time for rest.

The effect on mental work is more doubtful. When mind and body are exhausted by over-work and want of food, alcohol no doubt restores the power of free thought, and removes mental preoccupation. This it does in the way which we have already described, by quickening the circulation in the brain, and by its slight narcotic and deliriant properties. When taken with food it is not easy to decide how much of the effect is due to the food alone. But whilst there is no doubt that in many conditions alcohol does for a time promote the flow of thought and idea, it diminishes the power of clear and consecutive reasoning, and its use is nearly always followed by greater exhaustion and less power of application. One may perhaps make an exception in the case of public speaking for some length of time, where there is, in addition to thought, a physical strain and some excitement; alcohol does, in some cases of this kind, enable great mental efforts to be performed.

The conclusion is, then, that in ordinary life, only so much alcohol as is of use to insure mental rest and good digestion should be taken. Where these are sufficient without alcohol, none should be taken.

Under exceptional circumstances, such as exposure to cold or heat, or extraordinary exertion, is alcohol beneficial? Perhaps the best possible test is afforded by experience in the army. It is the almost unanimous experience of those who have given special attention to the question, that so far from being an aid to great exertion, and to the resistance of extremes of temperature, alcohol acts injuriously; and that such conditions are far better supported without it.*

The belief that alcohol produces warmth, and is therefore to be used on all occasions when there is a liability to chill, is one of the most common of popular errors, or, at least, is so regarded by scientific men. For experiments have shown that the principal action of alcohol is to lower the temperature of the body, in proportion to the quantity taken. It is a well-known fact that the human body (like that of all animals) has a certain temperature, which it maintains, with very slight variations, under the varied conditions of external temperature. Thus it has been shown that in the tropics and in the extremest cold there is a scarcely perceptible difference in the heat of the body, so long as health is maintained. This tempera-

---

* For further details on this interesting subject, which space forbids us from entering into, see the following:—Parkes on 'Hygiene,' fourth edition, p. 281; 'Medical Sketches of the Expedition to Egypt,' by Sir James M'Gregor, p. 86; Hamilton's 'Military Surgery,' p. 61: Sir John Hall, 'Medical History of the War in the Crimea,' vol. i. p. 504; 'Journal of the United Service Institution,' 1871, vol. xv. p. 74; Captain Huyshe's 'Account of the Red River Expedition'; 'Blackwood's Magazine,' Jan. 1871, p. 64; 'The Soldier's Pocket Book,' by Sir Garnet Wolseley, second edition, 1871, p. 172; Dr. W. B. Carpenter on 'The Physiology of Temperance and Total Abstinence,' 1870.

ture is about 98½° Fahrenheit; slightly lower in hot than in cold climates, owing to greater cooling by evaporation. This uniform heat of the body is essential for the healthy maintenance of nutrition, and appears to be regulated by the nervous system; that is, the various processes which go on in the body to produce heat, or to get rid of it, are under nervous control. A large number of diseases cause this regular heat to be deranged, and the body becomes too hot or too cool; and alcohol, like several other drugs, has the power of lowering the temperature, as will also the external application of cold to such an extent as to overcome the power of heat production in the body.

Alcohol, in a dose of any amount, has also the power of lowering considerably the general heat of the body below the natural standard, and in drunken persons very low temperatures indeed have been found. We do not yet know exactly how this effect is produced; some think it is by an action upon the central controlling part of the nervous system, just as we may derange the regulated filling of a cistern by holding up the ball-cock, or the rate of a steam-engine by checking the governor-balls. Others believe that it acts as a damper, preventing the proper burning of the substance which is found in the liver, and produces heat by combustion in the lungs. Whichever is the true view, there is no doubt about the action. But this is not quite the whole truth, for careful observation has shown that quite at first, when only a moderate dose of alcohol is taken, there is a slight rise in the body-temperature to the amount of $1°$ to $1\frac{1}{2}°$ Fahr., which lasts for a short time.

We must understand, however, that the temperature of all parts of the body is not the same, for different parts are more exposed to external cooling agencies. The skin of the arms and legs is always colder, usually many degrees colder, than the blood, and the parts immediately beneath the skin are cooler than the deeper parts. In fact, the temperature of any given part will depend on the free circulation of the warm blood from the interior of the body, and the absence of external cooling agencies. We can freeze the foot or hand by a freezing mixture, or warm it by exercise or rubbing, which make the circulation more active in it. In fact, we may regard it as one of the very important functions of the blood to act like a system of hot-water pipes, and keep all parts of our bodily house warm. The longer the warm blood stays at the parts most exposed the more is it cooled; the faster it is changed for fresh warm blood the better it keeps up its heat.

Now this is what alcohol really does in the body, and in many cases what we want it especially for. It widens the channels through which the blood flows, and thus lets the blood course more freely through them, and it quickens the beat of the heart, and sends more blood through in a given time. Moreover, cold of itself contracts the vessels, and makes them resist the passage of the blood; so that we see that alcohol directly counteracts the local effects of cold.

Now, what is the effect of a chill, such as from riding in the cold, getting wet feet, &c.? The danger seems to lie in this, that the blood-vessels of some part of the body, especially of some internal organ, owing to the impression made by the cold upon the surface, become affected, and thus a congestion and inflammation is set up. (The complete explanation is too technical to introduce here.) Now, although the effect of alcohol in any large quantity may be injurious, it is quite possible and probable that in a moderate one it may for a time do good, for it not only acts upon the vessels of the part chilled, but upon those of the internal organs, and thus makes the circulation everywhere more rapid and easy. For the evil effect of a chill is not in the lowering of the general temperature so much as in the local result, and its secondary effects on other parts.

When, however, we have to do with exposure to a cold climate or a very hot one, the question is very different. The habitual use of alcohol lowers the power of resistance to cold or heat, that is, it interferes with the central controlling authority, and so works mischief.

Old people who suffer from a languid circulation, cold feet and hands, and the like, are often benefited by alcohol, for example, spirits and water at night; because the blood-vessels have become degenerated and rigid, the heart weakened and unable to overcome the resistance in the vessels. Alcohol both aids in dilating the small vessels and quickening and invigorating the heart's action, and thus equalises the circulation, and allows the warm blood to flow freely in all parts of the body, so that the warmth of the more distant parts is maintained.

We may, then, use alcohol for this purpose of equalising heat and circulation in some cases, both for a time under exceptional circumstances, and habitually in moderate doses, where, either from defective action of the heart or a degenerated condition of the vessels, we cannot keep up the due balance of action. But we must remember that there are dangers attending the use of alcohol which should make us always prefer other means for attaining these ends, and that the dose must be strictly regulated by the necessity of the case. It is better that a man should suffer from cold feet than that by putting alcohol into him we should make the heart act so forcibly as to burst a vessel in his brain; and better that he should have a rather languid circulation, than that he should set up disease of his vessels and organs by constant use of alcohol. We may work a new and sound boiler at high pressure, but we must be careful how we increase the pressure when the boiler is rusty and the pipes furred. In many such cases of languid circulation, rest in a recumbent posture does all the good which alcohol could do, without its attendant dangers. Sufficiently frequent feeding and proper clothing must also be attended to.

Alcohol as a Stimulant.—Before we ask whether alcohol is a stimulant, we ought to inquire what we mean by the word. A stimulus is something which acts as a spur or whip, and rouses up some flagging energy. Does alcohol do this? Many people have said that it does not—that it only paralyses the higher controlling centres and lets the lower act. But whatever theory we may adopt, no one can doubt that somehow, under some conditions, a glass of wine does revive the energies, that it quickens the heart's action and the sluggish circulation, at any rate for a time.

No doubt, in many cases, even, perhaps, in most, this over-action is followed by corresponding depression; there is drowsiness, confusion of thought, languor, sluggish alimentary action, especially if the stimulation is at all more than absolutely necessary. So that some say that, on the whole, the stimulant effect adds nothing to the total income; it only temporarily overdraws the account at the banker's, and the deficit must be made up. But we do not think this to be absolutely true. Both for a time, in some healthy persons, and constantly in many who have no actual evident disease but a defective vital action, the use of alcohol is justifiable and desirable; so long as only so much is taken as to give the needed stimulus and no more. Chronic diseases require chronic remedies, and so do chronic defects of action.

The effects produced by alcohol in certain diseases show beyond a doubt that it has a certain action upon the nervous system, which we can only call stimulant or tonic. Especially is this seen in some cases of delirium in fever, and in failure of the heart's action in some acute diseases. In such cases alcohol is sometimes used in very large and repeated doses with only a good effect, and without any subsequent depression. It is idle to ignore the results of experience in disease; they are, so to speak, only the same on a very large and visible scale as those which occur in a less tangible form in the lesser derangements of health.

As a *sedative*, i.e. to promote rest and quiet, or sleep.— This, as we have seen, is the sequel of the former effect, and is produced mainly by the action upon the higher nervous centres, which can be temporarily paralysed by alcohol. In ordinary life, however, such a use of alcohol would be highly mischievous; even in disease, the result can better be attained by other means. The use of wine or spirits to relieve pain, headache, neuralgia, and the like, is one of the greatest danger; and when from long continuance of the cause of pain the habit becomes constant, the diseases caused by alcohol are most certainly produced. Very often the pain is really caused by the use of the alcohol, and ceases on its withdrawal.

Yet there are exceptional conditions in which the sedative effect of alcohol in a moderate degree is of great value. This is especially the case where over-mental activity or excitement prevent sleep or hinder digestion. The over-exhausted brain is incapable of taking rest; sleep is obtained with difficulty owing to continual active yet useless thought; there is much dreaming and the sleep is broken; in the daytime there is drowsiness and languor; the appetite is gone. Now all these may result from the use of alcohol, but they may also arise when no alcohol is used, simply from mental exhaustion, and then a small quantity of alcohol taken regularly gives great relief. In a similar way, as we have said, by removing mental preoccupation, appetite and digestion may be improved.

In elderly persons the use of wine or spirits and water as a "nightcap" is very common, and in many cases beneficial; but very often some light food would have an equally good effect, and we believe that in most cases where it is really needed, some food should be taken with it.

It must, however, always be remembered, that in using alcohol as a stimulant or sedative, that is, distinctly for either of those objects, we are entering upon a course which is more or less pernicious. For the action is only temporary, and needs repetition, and there is no habit more likely to cause its own repetition than the taking of alcohol. We step in and interfere with nature, and if nature replies by reckoning upon our interference, we are perhaps in a worse case than before. If we accustom ourselves to boots and clothing, nature does not give us hard hoofs and a dense hairy covering. Our acquired habits are some of the strongest parts of ourselves.

Moreover, there is no doubt that we can do work beyond our right measure and standard for a time under the influence of alcohol; and although the limit as regards bodily work is soon reached, and less work is done, it is not so certainly the case with mental, and we may readily go beyond the point of safety, with consequent weakening of our powers.

One word with regard to the diminution of alcohol or its entire cessation after it has been used as a stimulant or sedative. Can it be done with safety? Unquestionably, if in a person in ordinary health, it may be withdrawn at once and entirely; in diseased or in old persons it must be done more gradually and cautiously. The cessation is often attended with great discomfort, great craving for a return to it; but this is no indication of injury by the withdrawal, it shows only a morbid condition created by drinking. We may say, indeed, that such a craving is of itself an indication that more had been taken than was needed. Persons who take only a moderate quantity usually suffer no discomfort or inconvenience from going without for a few days, though they may feel the better for returning to their habitual allowance.

CHAPTER V.

ALCOHOL IN ILL-HEALTH AND DISEASE.

WE have said a good deal about the effects of alcohol in various conditions of slight ill-health, and it may be gathered from what we have already said that the habitual use of alcohol is *necessary* only when there is some departure from health. If it is only the daily friction of mental worry or bodily fatigue which is relieved by the daily use of a small quantity with food, just as grease relieves the friction of the wheels of a carriage, it is the slight degree of overwear or friction of the system which makes us need it. Now there are many conditions of ill-health in which alcohol is supposed to be beneficial, and it is one of the most difficult tasks of the doctor, and of those who wish to be guided by reason alone, to decide whether in such or such a case alcohol shall be taken, and in what form.

It would be waste of time to go into all these various conditions, and to try to suggest the appropriate modicum for each. Patients generally expect the doctor to tell them exactly how much stimulant, of what kind, and at what time, they are to take. Some follow blindly and exactly the instructions given, and this very wisely; others hedge a good deal, they take less or more as their inclination tends. If people would deal fairly and honestly with themselves, they could often judge far better than the doctor what is good for them. People often ask the doctor such a question as this: "Do you think three or four glasses of sherry a day would do me harm?" If he says, "Yes, take only two," the chances are that they will still take as much as before; if he says "No," they will take it too, though all the while knowing that it does harm them. In a large majority of cases the truest answer is, "You can judge far better yourself, both what form agrees with you best, and how much you really need; take that form which you can digest, and as little of it as possible." Men are too willing to leave others to judge for them, especially when the advice jumps with their own inclination, and they need to be brought honestly to use their own reason and act on their own responsibility.

Knowledge of the individual and his habits, of the tendencies of certain states of constitution, and the like, do, however, often enable the doctor to form an accurate judgment as to what is best.

Certain constitutions do not tolerate certain forms of stimulants, and some are always injured by alcohol. Every one knows that gouty people should not take young port, or sweet wines; that many dyspeptics cannot take ale or stout; that elderly persons often cannot take claret, and so on. Some of these difficulties are due to the other bodies, such as sugar, salts, &c., contained in the various liquors. But we could not go into all these points in a work like the present, and no one but a doctor could be expected fully to appreciate the minute shades of difference if we did. If one man finds that beer gives him dyspepsia or headache, and claret does not—if port flushes his face and makes him feel stupid, and champagne does not—if, in fact, one thing suits him and the other does not, he does not want a doctor to tell him which to take, so long as he possesses any amount of his reasoning faculties; but he may need to be told that he would be far better without any at all.

We must rather try to indicate what states of health show that alcohol as such is injurious or beneficial.

"Indigestion" is one of the common complaints for which alcohol is used. "Take a little wine for thy stomach's sake" is a very old prescription, but wanting in explicity both as to the quantity and nature of the wine. There are many forms of indigestion—one of the commonest in some classes is actually caused by alcohol, as we have already said. For this *the* remedy is entire abstention. So, too, when the water is high-coloured and loaded in the morning, the tongue coated, much thirst, drowsiness and heaviness during the day, the bowels sluggish, dull aching in the right side, &c., we may strongly suspect over-indulgence in the pleasures of the table, both in meat and drink, and counsel abstinence in both, and more exercise. But when there is loss of appetite, with a pale clean tongue, slight pain after food, capricious likings and loathings, and other symptoms showing difficulty in digestion in a person not in the habit of taking alcohol, it may often be given with food with very great advantage. We come back, however, to our starting point, that every case must be judged on its own merits, that other treatment should in most cases be employed, and that the kind and quantity of stimulant is to be regulated by the doctor's advice and the person's own experience. "Indigestion" is only a name for a condition varying widely in its causes and symptoms. It may easily be aggravated by the use of alcohol, or by use of it in the wrong form, or at wrong times, or it may be greatly relieved by it, and we should lead into error if we tried to go too much into detail. Experience is after all the best guide in any individual case, but an honest trial of total abstinence is always well worth making.

We may lay it down as a universal rule that if alcohol is to benefit digestion it must be taken with or soon after meals, that only a moderate quantity such as we have already indicated must be taken, and that the form must be regulated by experience. Beyond these general maxims we cannot here afford space to lay down any fixed rules.

Neuralgia in all its varied forms, and nerve pains of whatever kind, are generally supposed to demand the use of alcohol. It is here that the narcotic effect of alcohol is most frequently sought. If we go through the whole series of pains and aches to which our human frame is subject we shall find hardly one in which alcohol has not been recommended as a specific. Toothache, tic-douloureux, headache, &c., are often treated with large doses of brandy or port wine, and in many cases with great benefit, at least for a time. Alcohol has in such cases a double action; it makes the sensation of pain less by deadening the sensibility of the brain, and probably also it acts upon the vessels of the affected part, changes the relations of the vessels and nerves, and so alters and possibly relieves the pain. But in many cases, though it gives relief for a time, the pain returns with renewed vigour, and more alcohol must be taken, and so on. It is the nature of all nerve pains to come and go, and to be aggravated by diseased or unhealthy conditions of the general system, and unless there be some serious direct irritation of the nerve, to last only for a certain time and then go away. When pain is very severe and agonising, it is on all accounts desirable to relieve it, for nothing is more wearying to the human frame than severe pain. And for this we may use alcohol if we have no better means of relief, but we ought fully to understand why we use it. It is not to cure, and we may have to reckon with the possibility of the general state which causes the pain being made worse.

It cannot be too clearly understood that most neuralgias have a general as well as a local cause. How many people do we see who suffer agonies from toothache or earache whenever they get overworked or out of health. Their teeth may be as rotten as touchwood, but so long as they are in good health they feel nothing amiss; give them a few days' overwork, want of sleep, or anxiety, and they hurry to the dentist to have their teeth drawn. Now in very many such cases the amount of alcohol which relieves pain gives rise to dyspepsia, or to subsequent debility, and so indirectly aggravates the suffering.

We are not speaking here of the local use of alcohol in the form of brandy or rum, which sometimes has a very good effect in the relief of pain, e.g., in a tooth, or applied to the face in neuralgia. This use is a harmless one, too well known as a homely remedy to need recommendation here.

What we have said of the use of alcohol in severe acute neuralgia applies with greater force to its employment in long-standing or recurrent pain, and indeed nearly all chronic nervous diseases. In no condition is the use of alcohol so likely to become dangerous, and to make the mind and body slaves to it. This is equally true of the real bodily pains and discomforts to which so many are subject, and those mental pains which, like dank vapours, arise from the body and becloud the mind and soul. For those who really suffer pain of body find that drinking for a time relieves their sense of misery, but only so long as the alcohol is acting; when it has ceased they are as bad as, or worse than, ever, so that they again seek the bottle. By degrees they find that they need more frequent and larger doses to relieve their pain and discomfort, nor can they be for any length of time without it; and so from occasional small doses they slide into constant tippling. Soon they find that when they are not drinking they have not only their original pain but the malaise and wretchedness which result from alcohol itself, and they must take more to remove their sense of complicated misery. Thus from moderate drinkers, using alcohol in a strictly medicinal way, they become by degrees habitual drunkards, and ruin their health, constitution, and entire well-being, physical and moral.

Hypochondriacal and "nervous" people, who are readily "hipped," whose lives are made wretched by a sense of misery which has no external or evident cause, are often led into drinking. But they only aggravate and extend their wretchedness, and may say—

> "Sad once were we
> In the sweet air made gladsome by the sun;
> Now in these murky settlings are we sad."

They had to start with too little control over their sensations and feelings, and what they had they lose; and thus the soul

> "Yields her body to a fiend,
> Who after moves and governs it at will,
> 'Till all its time be rounded."

Whatever benefit there may be in the use of alcohol to "one that is of sorrowful heart" for a time, there is the greatest danger in it to those who are so by nature and habit; when once they begin to use it they become gradually enslaved, and the craving for drink is the tangible form which their longing for some relief takes on. They may, it is true, in like manner become slaves to opium or other narcotics, but it is rarely that they do not take spirits too, either at the same time or alternately with opium or morphia.

At some periods of life there is an especial tendency to drinking, owing to abnormal or morbid sensations caused by altered functional states. One of the most dangerous of these is the change of life in women, and it is at this period that many previously sober and moral women become addicted to drinking, often in secret at first, and lay the foundation of habits which shorten the life and degrade the character. No doubt this tendency is encouraged by custom and the influence of bad advice, but, in many cases, there is a very strong inclination towards drinking which needs nothing but the possibility of secret gratification to cause it to be indulged in. Those who have not had the opportunities which doctors unfortunately enjoy of hearing the sad revelations which are sometimes made on this subject, would be astonished at the amount of secret drinking amongst apparently respectable and sober middle-aged women.

In the state of maternity and childbirth the same is true to an enormous extent. The amount of drinking which is carried on, both at these times and by nursing mothers, under a wrong idea of the necessity for alcohol, and an entire misconception of its true action, is almost beyond belief. On no subject connected with drinking is it more necessary to speak emphatically, for the direct and indirect effects of such a misuse are evils of incalculable extent. It seems to have become one of the doctrines and tenets of the female world that alcohol is essential to women who are nursing, and that it is not only a benefit to them, but their duty to take a considerable quantity. If this error were confined to the lower classes we might not be surprised, but unfortunately it is equally common in the higher. Monthly nurses are probably more chargeable with spreading drunkenness among married women than any other class. Their position and supposed experience as " wise women " enable them to insinuate the temptation and propagate the error, in spite of all the efforts of doctors and moralists. Young mothers especially are led by their advice as if they were bound hand and foot ; and, in spite of their better judgment, they give way to their leaders in a hitherto unknown land, and blindly follow their blind guides.

The evil thus brought upon young married women is enormous, and the result in physical and moral deterioration is most saddening. But this is not by any means the sole evil effect, for the habit tells upon the offspring whom it is intended to benefit. We are not speaking of the effect of drunkenness in the mother, which has terrible results in infant mortality or life-long disease, but the result of drinking more than is habitual or moderate, the effect of which, though less in degree, is of the same kind; and there is the strongest probability that the moral and mental character of children is influenced by the action of alcohol in the mother, and greater misery thus caused than even by crippling or fatal disease.

There is no evidence that alcohol is more necessary or beneficial to mothers, as such, and all experience points strongly in the opposite direction; so that those who wish to preserve their own health, and the life and health of their children, should resist the bad advice so often pressed upon them, and avoid alcohol as much as possible.

Alcohol in Disease.—It may be thought that we have said very little as to the use of alcohol in disease. Most people, at any rate doctors, admit that alcohol is a most valuable drug, and those who have had to deal much with severe disease know of what immense value it is in many cases. We have mentioned some of the slighter ailments in which it is useful, but beyond this we must not go here. For whilst alcohol may be used with great benefit, and in very large doses in some diseases, the knowledge of how and when to use it with profit is one of these points which require all the special skill and experience of the physician, and the indications for its use require technical knowledge which we could not here impart. It is especially in acute diseases and fevers, and in some diseases of the nervous system and heart, that it finds its greatest use; but in such cases it should always be given as a medicine in carefully measured doses, and at stated times, and never left to the discretion either of the nurse or the patient. Nor let it be imagined that caprice or educational bias is the guide of the doctor in giving or withholding alcohol; there is no drug the effects of which in disease have been more minutely and scientifically investigated of late years than alcohol, and a great mass of accurate knowledge as to its effects is the result; so that he who pretends that giving alcohol is merely a matter of conjecture or routine is either an ignoramus or a quack.

And, lastly, the common use of brandy in all sorts of ailments, as a specific, cannot be too earnestly deprecated. It is quite true that in many slight ailments it gives relief, and in some is very useful when no other remedy is at hand; for example, in colic or diarrhœa, in exhaustion or fainting, in shock from accident, and the like. We have purposely avoided discussing its use under these circumstances, because we are convinced that there is no need to mention all the conditions which may call for it, and that what needs to be said is more in the way of caution than advice. For in a very large number of cases, the giving of brandy actually does harm, in many others it does no good, and obscures the true nature of the case when the doctor is called in. A man is seen to reel and stagger in the street; the bystanders gather round him; he complains of being sick and faint, perhaps falls and becomes partially unconscious. The two things which kind neighbours or good Samaritans do are, first to try to help him to stand up, and then to fetch him some brandy, or to support him to the nearest public-house to get some, and then pour down a large quantity. And thus many a case of commencing apoplexy has been aggravated and made fatal; or a man with heart or brain disease taken to a police-cell as drunk, and died there. We believe that in by far the majority of cases the rough-and-ready treatment of ignorant persons has thus been absolutely injurious; in very few beneficial.

The use of spirits has often been supposed to aid in preventing the attacks of fever, ague, and other infectious and malarial diseases. The experience on this point derived from army statistics seems to show that alcohol has no effect in warding off malarial fever, cholera, or dysentery. Nor does its presence promote attack. Yellow fever is peculiarly fatal to intemperate persons. With regard to other fevers, we have no evidence that they are at all prevented by alcohol, and they are certainly, like nearly all other diseases, more fatal in persons who have indulged to excess than in others.

CHAPTER VI.

THE RIGHT USE OF ALCOHOL.

WE have thus briefly discussed the various uses and abuses of alcohol ; and from what we have said, it is evident that alcohol has a right use, as an article of diet and as a medicine ; but that it may be easily misused through ignorance of its action, as well as from wilful indulgence

Upon the dietetic use of alcohol we cannot do better than quote the words of the late lamented Dr. Parkes, which will meet with the concurrence of all right-thinking men.

"The dietetic value of alcohol has been much overrated. It does not appear to me possible at present to condemn altogether alcohol as an article of diet in health ; or to prove that it is invariably hurtful, as some have attempted to do. It produces effects which are often useful in disease, and sometimes desirable in health ; but in health it is certainly not a necessity, and many persons are much better without it. As now used by mankind it is infinitely more powerful for evil than good."

It is only needful now briefly to gather together some hints as to the mode in which alcohol should be used, if at all.

Choice of a Beverage.—First in order comes the choice of a beverage. We cannot attempt to prescribe the right kind of alcoholic stimulant for each individual. We have shown that each has its own peculiar properties; that the most healthful and least injurious forms are those which contain alcohol in the smallest quantity, and in the most combined form. Spirits are directly injurious to the tissues with which they come in contact, and cause destruction of other organs most rapidly; hence their habitual use is only to be permitted when necessitated by disease, or when there is absolute incapacity to tolerate any other form. Wines have their especial use in relation to digestion and nutrition; the stronger wines form a class quite distinct from the lighter in this respect. For ordinary use the lighter wines alone should be taken, those having less than 10 per cent. of alcohol being preferable, and ale or stout being still more advantageous, as affording nutriment, and tonic and digestive principles in addition.

Beyond these general principles, the selection must be determined by individual constitution.

Quantity of Alcohol.—The quantity daily should not exceed half-an-ounce of *absolute alcohol*, and even this is a limit which should not be reached if less can be taken. To take one ounce daily is to reach nearly the limit of diminished power, and it goes beyond the bounds of safe stimulation. We must here refer to what we have already said (see p. 12) as to the quantity of various liquors which contain this amount.

Summary of Conclusions.

1. In *health* the use of alcohol is unnecessary, and its habitual employment is liable to produce disease, hence total abstinence is the safest course.

2. When the *habitual* use of alcoholic beverages in some form is found necessary, the following rules are to be observed:—

The *quantity* must be the least possible, and usually not more than that containing half-an-ounce of absolute alcohol per diem.

The *form* should always be dilute, and the alcohol in a state of intimate combination. Wines containing more than 10 per cent. of alcohol should not be drunk undiluted.

The *time* should be always with meals, preferably only with dinner; never in the morning or between meals.

3. In very many cases where alcoholic beverages may be used temporarily with advantage no definite rules can

be laid down other than those given in the preceding pages. But let the dangers, moral, social, and physical, of excess in drinking always be borne in mind, and control the action in this matter.

4. In *disease* alcohol should be used only as a medicine, and the quantity, quality, and time strictly regulated by the doctor's orders.

If these rules, and the principles upon which they are grounded were observed, we should not have to lament the ruin of health and constitution, and the increase of vice and crime which now result from excessive drinking.

W. S. GREENFIELD.

LIST OF PRINCIPAL AUTHORITIES FOR REFERENCE.

Anstie, Dr. F. E. On Stimulants and Narcotics. London, 1864.
———. On the Use of Wines in Health and Disease. London, 1877.
Carpenter, Dr. W. B., F.R.S. The Physiology of Temperance and Total Abstinence. London, 1870.
Huss-Magnus. Alcoholismus Chronicus.
Magnan, Dr. V. On Alcoholism. (Translation.) London, 1876.
Parkes, Dr. E. A., F.R.S. On Hygiene. Fourth edition, 1873, p. 279 *et seq.*
———. Personal Care of Health.
Richardson, Dr. B. W., F.R.S. On Alcohol.
Report of Committee of Convocation of Canterbury on Intemperance.
Report of the Committee of the House of Lords on Intemperance.

www.ingramcontent.com/pod-product-compliance
Lightning Source LLC
Chambersburg PA
CBHW032242080426
42735CB00008B/967